Girl, Drowning

by

Dana Knott

YELLOW ARROW
PUBLISHING

Baltimore, Maryland, USA

Girl, Drowning
Copyright © 2026 by Yellow Arrow Publishing
All rights reserved.

Library of Congress Control Number: 2026937783
ISBN (paperback): 978-1-967202-02-7

The interior images were created by Elizabeth Eleanor Siddal (1829–1862) in the 19th century and retrieved from Wikimedia Commons (commons.wikimedia.org); more information can be found in the back of the book.

Cover art and design by Alexa Laharty (Instagram @alexaelisabeth). Interior design by Yellow Arrow Publishing. For more information, see yellowarrowpublishing.com.

In memory of Elizabeth Eleanor Siddal

~

In love for Kip and Callum

~

In gratitude to Dr. Gregory Scholtz

~

In recognition of Dr. Jan Marsh and author Lucinda Hawksley

Contents

GIRL, DROWNING

Girl, Drowning

Ophelia, John Everett Millais, 1851–1852

What does he know
about the pathology
of a heart in a drowning girl
whose red hair radiates
like *Polysiphonia*?

He once saw the body
of a lovely suicide
who had jumped
from the Bridge of Sighs
into the River Thames.

What does he know
about this strange, quiet
girl who poses in a tin
bath of brackish city water
from a suicide's lungs?

She floats, transfixed,
like a statue of ice
glazed in silver and frost,
the oil lamps extinguished,
the water winter-cold.

What does he know
about a girl's thoughts before
drowning? To accept fate
and sing the final notes
that will die between her lips?

The girl will look at herself
horrified, fascinated, as if
staring into a crystal ball
from which death emerges,
a blazing scarlet poppy.

Supermodel

Stand slender as a brush stroke.
Silence the mind and still the body.
Let the heart mimic the grave
beats of a windup metronome.

Embrace the romantic disease,
pale skin and blushing cheeks
heightened by acid red hair,
the beauty of consumptive chic.

Be the muse, the object of desire,
Beatrice Portinari, a divine revelation,
a virgin among working class whores,
a crimson dove among the wolves.

Become the tragic figure. Love
an unworthy man. Give in to art's
demands and count the acrid drops,
like days, until the suicidal end.

Lady Clare, ca. 1854–1857

The First Dose

It was opium
before opioids,
Papaver somniferum,
the bringer of sleep
and strange dreams.

Laudanum, a tincture
of opium, Victorian
cure-all in cocktail form
for teething babies
and troubled women.

The alcoholic burn,
the taste of saffron,
vanilla, or orange peel
from an emerald
green apothecary bottle.

The doctor said, "Open."
I was nothing but obedient.
He placed the bitter drops
onto my invalid tongue.
"Take as needed," he said.

I stared at the copper
ceiling tiles. My hands lifted,
reaching for the dying stars
blooming like peonies
in blues and red.

Art Lessons

He says I have a natural talent.
He is my teacher and I his
pupil who borrows his pencils.

He advises, "Drop the second L
in your name. One L is more
refined." So I am Siddal now.

He guides my unsure hand across
the canvas. His soft beard tickles
my skin like a plush sable brush.

I stay in his rooms to practice,
to soften the stiffness of my figures.
Soon he gives me lessons in bed.

Between my small breasts my heart
beats *please* and *more*, hungers
like an addict. I am a summer field

of fresh-cut hay, warm and sweet
and intoxicating. As we tremble
together, he says, "Look at me."

But how can I gaze into those eyes
again? Instead, I look above his head.
Dust motes silvered by moonlight

fall like tiny stars at the world's end.

Artistic Study

I study his hands pulling apart a loaf of bread.
I study the movement of his jaw as he chews.
I watch his enjoyment of an aged whisky,

how he strokes his beard while composing
a sonnet in his head. I know the amused
smile that forms when he catches my stare

from across the room. How he waits for me
to notice his desire and lead him to our bed.
I memorize the smell of his skin, a mingling

of salt, turpentine, and wood smoke.
I worship at the altar of his body, breathe
him in and marvel at the sorcery of his touch.

Love has the power to transform a man into a god.
When he leaves me drifting toward a dream,
I wonder when he will return to being a man.

Drawing His Likeness, 1853

For one rare moment he sits for me,
hands in coat pockets, legs crisscrossed
on the seat of the chair between us.

I look past his condescending eyes,
his stare, his Medusa-like glare,
his smile a mere muscle away from a sneer.

I am mesmerized by his uncivilized hair
as I tease out the threads of his beard
in pencil. How many times in a feverish

high has he drawn me? Lizzie in repose,
Lizzie reading, sewing a dress, gazing
upon his face. So many Lizzies

flower throughout our rooms, overflow
from dresser drawers. He is restless.
I blow the graphite from my drawing board.

He unfreezes his body and walks
behind me. He peers over my shoulder.
"Is it a good likeness?" I ask,

and he simply kisses the top of my head.

Self-Portrait

I am no Helen of Troy.
I am no destroyer of cities.

I do not flatter myself
as some great beauty.

I am more pigeon than dove,
a plague rather than a prayer.

My long neck is not the neck
of a swan, but a pedestal

holding the face of a nun,
pale, fallen, forgotten.

Verdant green mutes the red
of my hair like a veil.

The heavy lids below my brows
hide the blue bruises of my eyes

but not the weary truth
of how I see my imperfect self.

Art lies in artifice.
My lover is a liar.

Pippa Passes, 1854

Aspiring Poet

What do I have to write about? Love?
I write only what I know, simple,
courtly poems full of indelible sorrows
and simple rhymes: dead, true, red, blue.

My cramped hand, its ink-spotted fingers,
scribbles words smudged, almost illegible,
like a verse of Tennyson I found wrapped
around a butter pat, reduced to domestic use.

I know these fragile creatures will not thrive.
I gave myself to parasitic love. I have little
blood to feed them. What I create always dies,
my creations delicate like blown glass that shatters

even from the resonance of a sigh.

Mistress

"She is a stunner and no mistake. Rossetti once told
me that, when he first saw her, he felt his destiny was
defined. Why does he not marry her?"

from a diary entry of Ford Madox Brown, March 10, 1855

I have tried to step out of time and enter
some place, unfettered, that belongs
only to him and me, where we belong
only to each other. Always I am alone
in my soporific haze, envisioning him
apart from me, free with other women.

I have tried to freeze us in one perfect
moment, a walk together along the Thames,
or the first time we made love in his studio.
I wore a loose, medieval gown, its fabric
the color of an English wolf. He grasped
its hem to draw over my head.

I stood naked before him, no tightly laced
corset to untie, my body languid as a willow
bowing over the river. Like Narcissus,
I was adrift, mesmerized by my own reflection
in his water-blue eyes. I thought I might die
from shame or desire and hid my face

behind my flowing red hair. But then I felt
his closeness, the prayer of his palms
against the small slope of my breasts, my belly
as flat as a table waiting to be set by his body.
My mind lost all thought, all fear, all warning.
I am his, but I am not his. Most times

I am the mistress dressed in a quilted tunic,
cold, aloof, sometimes witty, always sarcastic.
I belong to just myself until I am claimed
by my addictions and kept inside,
assigned to bed to avoid embarrassment.
The English wolf has been hunted to extinction.

Solitude

Your shadow has followed you
out the door. I remain alone,
lying next to the impression
of your body in the sheets
as if I lie with a ghost of a man.
Too tired to turn the pages,
I yearn for your lips to shape
the words, your gentle voice
to soothe my ears with poetry.
I never knew such loneliness
until I knew your tenderness.
How you warmed my feet
between your paint-stained
hands or traced the wingspan
of my collarbone with a brush.
I know your secret, that you are
with her. I know that you crave
her ample flesh as my form wastes
away. I am left to satisfy my own
craving, a testament to solitude,
the pale full moon in a starless sky,
a solitary pair of footprints in snow,
coppery stray hairs on your pillow.

Pre-Raphaelite Death Cult

I was his dove, his Sid, his beloved
Guggums. I was his muse.
Gabriel painted me as Francesca

and himself as Paolo, adulterous
lovers damned to Hell's eternity.
Expectation damned me.

Destiny never demands fidelity.
I was his faithful, hysterical patient,
bedridden for days, thin, weak,

too ill to eat, demanding his attention.
He left me for warmer company,
voluptuous, robust, willing women,

street whores or the wives of friends.
There is a special circle in Hell
for women who hurt other women.

I was never a saintly, sexless creature.
I was once his instrument for pleasure.
Dying is not erotic. It is not ecstatic.

It is so much pain, isolation, and terror.
He will see sensuality in my agony,
and I will be such a beautiful corpse.

Miss Siddal Thinks of Leaving

The bird refuses to sing.
It mirrors my own silence.
I open the silver door,
but it remains on its perch.
I could throw off the covers,
pull my body from its bed,
my legs heavy, the floor cold.
I hate to think of each icy step.

I take tiny sips from my glass
and surround myself
with a golden mist.

I dream of leaving,
but I wake
in his arms. I never heard
his strong steps on the stairs
or the turn of the key in the door.

Clerk Saunders (study 1), ca. 1854–1857

A Pre-Raphaelite Exhibition

"Her drawings display an admiring adoption of all
the most startling peculiarities of Mr. Rossetti's style,
but they have nevertheless qualities which entitle
them to high praise."

an exhibition review by Coventry Patmore, July 4, 1857

I. For Art's Sake

I was not the Angel of the House,
although he called me his dove.

I was more than the passive girl
freezing to death in a bathtub.

I kept him as much as he kept me.
He said that I was his destiny.

I was his muse and later his wife.
I was never the love of his life.

He consumed me to sustain his art.
A student often imitates her tutor.

I bought my own colors and brushes
but confused painting with daydreams.

I tossed a coin in a Roman wishing well.
How terrifying when wishes come true.

II. *Clerk Saunders* by Elizabeth Eleanor Siddal*

He said it was the best of my paintings.
Still, they all looked for his hand

in my brushstrokes. I knew the heartbreak
of the murder ballad's red-haired Margaret

and her lover's ghost, how he refused her wish
for a final kiss because one kiss from the dead

would kill as quickly as a breeze that lifts
the bright strands of her hair. Yet he pleaded

with her to set him free. Her face was ghostly
pale as she enchanted a branch with her kiss

to release his spirit from his lover's vow.
And for her troubles he made her promise

never to love another as much as she loved him.
Whether I was Margaret or the ghost, I did not know.

But I was the only woman in the show.

* Siddal based *Clerk Saunders* on an old Scottish ballad of the same
name. For more information, see the back of the book.

Wedding Day, May 23, 1860

I am so weary.
I am too weary to weep.

Grief requires energy.
My wrist barely throbs a pulse.

I can barely lift my lids,
as if my eyes have been covered

with farthings by mourners.
Please. I am not ready

for the ground. Let me stay
to dream of crystal palaces

and stained glass windows.
My sheet is not yet my shroud.

Rewind the little silver clock
and let its pendulum swing.

He has heard of my dying
and now sits by my bedside.

"If you can find the strength
to live," he said. "I promise

to make you my bride."
And so I lived.

I wear a wreath of flowers,
a veil instead of graveclothes.

The mirror remains uncovered
and reflects my pale face.

He carries me to St. Clement's
and we whisper our vows

under glowing chandeliers.
At last, we are married.

We laugh like naughty children
and toss orange blossoms at each other.

I was once his model, his muse.
Now I am his wife.

How heavy his ring
rests upon my finger.

Wedding Portrait

Regina Cordium, Dante Gabriel Rossetti, 1860

He sees me now for what I am
an invalid, a possessive creature
tinged with absinthe green,
the flush of fever on my cheeks.

I am a weary queen of hearts,
cascading hair for my crown,
heavy eyes absent of desire,
crimson lips with no hint of a smile.

A red coral necklace wraps around
my throat like a network of arteries,
but I am anemic, drained of lifeblood.
I do not hold the passionate rose.

I clasp a purple pansy, a delicate
flower with a face, from pensée,
to think and remember. What thoughts
will I gather like bouquets in my dreams?

Stillborn

"Lizzie has just been delivered of a dead child.
She is doing pretty well, I trust."

Dante Gabriel Rossetti, in a letter to his mother, May 2, 1861

Like Noah's dove, her soul left
my body even as her own
body remained in mine for days.

Once, her gentle fluttering
reassured my anxious mind.
Stillness is the herald of Death.

No hope nests in my torn heart.
To never feel her sweet breath,
her tiny lungs like folded wings.

Of her, I have only wispy hair,
feathery and red between
pages of a book. She is gone.

She is dead. I cradle nothing
but her empty nightdress.
He stands at the door, watching,

and opens his mouth to speak.
"Shhh. You'll wake the baby,"
I say as the room fills with birdsong.

Accidental Death

"Accidentally and casually and by misfortune."

Inquest into the death of Elizabeth Eleanor Rossetti

He will unpin the note from my breast,
read it, and toss my words into the fire.

He will fail to revive me with his embrace.
He will summon the first doctor to my bed.

When he asks, "Is there nothing you can do?"
the first doctor will reply, "She is lost to us."

He will summon a second doctor and a third.
The fourth doctor will pump my stomach.

The room will smell of brandy and sweet spices.
The tiny fetus will remain unborn in my womb.

My sister will run a damp cloth across my skin
and a silver brush through my tangled hair.

He will testify I was excitable. He will say I
was flighty. He will say, "She did not wish to die."

He will tell them, "She had a diseased heart.
She could not live without her hundred drops."

The Woeful Victory, 1860

Wake

From *Dante Gabriel Rossetti: His Family-Letters, with
a Memoir by William Michael Rossetti*

For days he kept watch over my body,
resting in an open casket above
a cooling board and its sheet of ice.
He could not believe I was dead.
"Come back to me, Lizzie," he said.

And in some unknown place, I heard.
"I am so cold, Gabriel, so very cold."
I spoke, but no cloud of breath
drifted from my parted blue lips.
Hopeful, he looked for signs of life

and called the doctor who, once
again, placed his fingers against
my neck and confirmed my death.
My sister clipped a lock of my hair,
my thin face pale in its halo of red.

If I should find Heaven, let it be
the woods flooded with bluebells,
their perfume fresh, leafy, and clean,
where we sought shelter from rain
and drank water from a sweet spring,

where he held me close and asked
me a question. I anointed him with
bluebells he called "witches' thimbles."
We carved our initials in willow trunks
and stones and at last in the window-

pane when we returned to our home.

Highgate Cemetery

"Also to the memory of Elizabeth Eleanor
wife of their elder son Dante Gabriel Rossetti
who died February 11th 1862 aged 30"

The inscription on the Rossetti family plot, Highgate Cemetery

I am the suicide in the Christian churchyard,
the pathetic lover, the shameful addict.

I am the interloper among dead Rossettis,
the ragged red wolf among the flock.

Against each waxy cheek sits a black book
like a raven, one, the Bible with its gilt edges,

the other, his poems, sustenance for the soul,
sustenance for the worms. In quiet decay,

my body rests in peace. My spirit, untethered
and restless, drifts like fog along London streets,

through the keyhole, and down dark hallways,
to his door. Each night I stand at the foot of his bed.

Before he died, he said, "Let me not on any account
be buried at Highgate," refusing to sleep by my side.

Wife of Rossetti

They built a bonfire large enough
to immolate the Maid of Lorraine

to illuminate my gravestone
and give the gravediggers light.

They told him I remained
beautiful and uncorrupted

even after seven years of sleep.
They told him my copper hair

had continued to grow wild,
as vibrant as a field of poppies.

And he wanted to believe them,
but his poems reeked of my death,

worms had riddled the pages with holes.
And I became the star of my own

macabre, tragic story. I began
as an enticing nereid in a tin tub

and ended as a body in a grave.

Acknowledgments

Thank you to the following publishers and journals for publishing earlier versions of some of the poems within Girl, Drowning:

Ethel Zine (print and online), August 2021
"Miss Siddal Thinks of Leaving"

FERAL: A Journal of Poetry and Art (print and online),
    October 1, 2021
"Girl, Drowning"

Trouvaille Review (online), April 18, 2022
"Aspiring Poet"

Green Ink Poetry (online), June 12, 2022
"Solitude"

Dodging the Rain (online), July 1, 2022
"Art Lessons," "Self Portrait," and "Stillborn"

The Orchards Poetry Journal (print), Summer 2022
"Highgate Cemetery"

A Sketch of Elizabeth Eleanor Siddal

Striking red hair, dreamy eyes, and willowy body, Elizabeth Eleanor Siddal (1829–1862) was the Pre-Raphaelite "it girl." In 1849, artist Walter Deverell "discovered" her working as a hat shop girl and enlisted her to become an art model, but Siddal already aspired to refine her raw artistic talent. She famously posed in a bathtub for John Everett Millais' *Ophelia* and became dangerously ill when the candles heating the water burned out. A founding member of the Pre-Raphaelite Brotherhood, Dante Gabriel Rossetti, claimed "Lizzie" as his exclusive muse and encouraged her development as an artist and poet. She was his "Guggums" and his dove.

Although he obsessively sketched portraits of her, Rossetti resisted marrying her due to class differences and his philandering ways. Siddal grew dependent on laudanum to treat her poor health, and her addiction enhanced her status as a tragic, pale beauty. Her art caught the eye of critic John Ruskin, who paid her £150 a year for her work. She wrote melancholic poems deemed too dark to publish. In 1857 Siddal achieved the distinction of being the only woman artist with work in the Pre-Raphaelite Exhibition.

Her relationship with Rossetti was a tumultuous one, punctuated by her illnesses, his infidelities, separations, and reconciliations. During one separation, Siddal attended art school in Sheffield, her creativity a constant presence. The couple reunited in 1860 when Rossetti heard that Siddal was on her deathbed. He carried her to church, and after 11 years, they finally married. Their marital happiness was brief as Siddal gave birth to a stillborn girl. She became pregnant again but feared another loss. On February 10, 1862, Rossetti found Siddal unresponsive, and despite the efforts of four doctors, Siddal died from a laudanum overdose in the early hours of February 11.

As a final romantic gesture, Rossetti placed a manuscript of his poetry in her coffin, only to have her exhumed seven years later to retrieve his poems. Legend had it that Siddal's body remained lovely and uncorrupted, her red hair filling the coffin For many years, her laudanum addiction, her fame as Ophelia in the bathtub, and her gruesome exhumation defined her. In recent years, due to the work of feminist scholars, Lizzie Siddal Rossetti now enjoys the critical appraisal she deserves as an artist and poet.

*****

Several references were used in the creation of Girl, Drowning, *including, generally:*

Hawksley, Lucinda. *Lizzie Siddal: Face of the Pre-Raphaelites*, 1st U.S. ed. Walker, 2006.

Marsh, Jan. *Elizabeth Siddal: Her Story*. Pallas Athene, 2023.

Marsh, Jan. *The Legend of Elizabeth Siddal*, 2nd ed. Quartet Books, 2010.

*****

Sources of quotes with specific poems, by order in the text:

With "Mistress"

Brown, Ford Madox. "10 March 1855." In *The Diary of Ford Madox Brown*, edited by Virginia Surtees. Yale University Press, 1981.

With "A Pre-Raphaelite Exhibition"

Patmore, Coventry. "A Pre-Raphaelite Exhibition." *Saturday Review*, July 4, 1857.

> In the old Scottish ballad "Clerk Saunders," Clerk Saunders is murdered by the brothers of his lover, Margaret. Siddal captures the moment when his ghost visits Margaret and asks her to release him from his vow of fidelity.

With "Stillborn"

Rossetti, Dante Gabriel. "2 May 1861." In *Dante Gabriel Rossetti: His Family-Letters, with a Memoir by William Michael Rossetti*. Vol. 2. Ellis and Elvey, 1895.

With "Accidental Death"

"Death of a Lady from an Overdose of Laudanum." *Daily News*, February 14, 1862.

With "Wake"
Rossetti, William Michael. "XXV. Death of Mrs. Dante
Rossetti." In *Dante Gabriel Rossetti: His Family-Letters, with
a Memoir by William Michael Rossetti*. Vol. 1. Ellis and Elvey,
1895.

With "Highgate Cemetery"
Quote pulled from a photograph of the tombstone in the
family plot in Highgate Cemetery West, section XIV, in
London.

✴✴✴✴✴

*Citations for the interior images (drawn by Elizabeth Eleanor Siddal),
by order in the text:*

Opposite "The First Dose"
Lady Clare, ca. 1854–1857. Pen, ink, and wash over graphite on
paper, 14.9 × 11.5 cm. Fitzwilliam Museum.
commons.wikimedia.org/wiki/File:Elizabeth_Siddal_-_Lady_
Clare.jpg

Opposite "Aspiring Poet"
Pippa Passes, 1854. Pen and brown ink on paper, 23.4 × 29.8 cm.
Ashmolean Museum.
commons.wikimedia.org/wiki/File:Elizabeth_Siddal_-_Pippa_
Passes.jpg

Opposite "A Pre-Raphaelite Exhibition"
Clerk Saunders (study 1), ca. 1854–1857. Pencil on paper, 8.9 ×
14 cm.
commons.wikimedia.org/wiki/File:Elizabeth_Siddal_-_Clerk_
Saunders_(study_1).jpg

Opposite "Wake"

The Woeful Victory, 1860. Ink and graphite on paper.
commons.wikimedia.org/wiki/File:Elizabeth_Siddal_-_The_
Woeful_Victory_(1).jpg

DANA KNOTT (she/her), born in Chicago, Illinois, resides in Delaware, Ohio, and works in Columbus as Director of Libraries at the Columbus State Library. She occasionally teaches a course she designed on storytelling and social justice at Antioch University. Knott holds an MA in English, an MA in library and information science, and an EdD in education for organizational leadership. She wrote the poems contained in *Girl, Drowning* during the COVID-19 lockdown, a disruptive yet surprisingly creative time when Knott also launched *tiny wren lit*, which publishes micropoetry online with downloadable zines for each issue. She has a sizable collection of various, old editions of *The Rubaiyat of Omar Khayyam* and a growing collection of Edward Gorey-signed books, first editions, and ephemera. Her work has appeared in *Yellow Arrow Journal's* **EMBLAZON** issue, *Bitter Oleander*, ONE ART, *FERAL: A Journal of Poetry and Art*, *The York Review*, *right hand pointing*, *Dust Poetry Magazine*, *Ethel Zine*, *Minerva Rising*, *Cosmic Daffodil*, *East Ridge Review*, and *Moss Puppy Magazine*. Her micro chapbook *Funeral Flowers* was published by Rinky Dink Press in 2024.

Thank you for supporting independent publishing.

Yellow Arrow Publishing is a nonprofit supporting writers and artists who identify as women. Visit YellowArrowPublishing.com for information on our publications, workshops, and writing opportunities.